Attack on America

The Day the Twin Towers Collapsed

Mary Gow

AMERICAN DISASTERS

Enslow Publishers, Inc.

40 Industrial Road   PO Box 38
Box 398   Aldershot
Berkeley Heights, NJ 07922   Hants GU12 6BP
USA   UK

http://www.enslow.com

This book is dedicated to all the men and women who lost their lives to terrorism on September 11, 2001.

Library of Congress Cataloging-in-Publication Data

Gow, Mary.
    Attack on America : the day the Twin Towers collapsed / Mary Gow.
        p. cm. -- (American disasters)
    Includes bibliographical references and index.
    Summary: An account of events surrounding the terrorist attacks that took place at the World Trade Center in New York City, at the Pentagon near Washington, D.C., and in rural western Pennsylvania on September 11, 2001.
    ISBN 0-7660-2118-1
    1. September 11 Terrorist Attacks, 2001—Juvenile literature. 2. Terrorism—New York (State)—New York—Juvenile literature. 3. Terrorism—United States—Juvenile literature. 4. Hijacking of aircraft—United States—Juvenile literature. [1. September 11 Terrorist Attacks, 2001. 2. Terrorism.] I. Title. II. Series.
    HV6432 .G68 2002
    973.931–dc21
                                          2001007613

Printed in the United States of America

10 9 8 7 6 5 4 3 2 1

To Our Readers:
We have done our best to make sure all Internet Addresses in this book were active and appropriate when we went to press. However, the author and the publisher have no control over and assume no liability for the material available on those Internet sites or on other Web sites they may link to. Any comments or suggestions can be sent by e-mail to comments@enslow.com or to the address on the back cover.

Illustration Credits: AP/Wide World Photos, pp. 8, 15, 16, 18, 19, 22, 24, 25, 27, 28, 30, 33, 34, 36, 38, 40, 42, 48, 49, 51; Corel Corporation, p. 4; David Torsiello/Enslow Publishers, Inc., pp. 43, 45, 52, 54; Kurt Weber/Enslow Publishers, Inc., p. 11.

Cover Illustration: AP/Wide World Photos.

225888 1

Contents

*T*he sun rises on the Twin Towers of the World Trade Center in lower Manhattan.

CHAPTER 1

September 11, 2001

September 11, 2001, started out like any other Tuesday at Logan International Airport in Boston. Claudia Richey, a security supervisor, stood at her post beside the metal detectors at Gate 19. It was 5:40 A.M. when a man with a small beard and mustache, carrying no bags, walked past her. He said nothing, keeping his hands in his pockets as he went through the metal detector. Richey stopped him, told him to take his hands out of his pockets and walk through again.

As he did, Richey studied the man's face. She thought he looked like a police sketch she had seen of a man accused of distributing hate leaflets in the Boston area. A coworker assured her that there was no resemblance. Richey let the man pass, wishing him a good flight as he walked away.[1]

Throughout the northeastern United States, alarm clocks were buzzing. People were getting up, showering, and eating breakfast. It was a beautiful day with hardly a cloud in the sky. At Logan Airport, just before eight o'clock, two Boeing 767 jets were taking off: American Airlines Flight 11 and United Airlines Flight 175. Both were bound for Los Angeles.

Labor Day had come and gone. Summertime was over. Children were on their way to school. In most New York City schools, it was the fourth day of classes. Students were still meeting classmates and learning their new teachers' routines.

On that Tuesday morning, hundreds of thousands of men and women in and around New York City were commuting to work. More than 40,000 of them were going to their jobs in the World Trade Center in downtown Manhattan.

The mayoral primaries were also taking place in New York City that day. A primary is when different political parties select candidates to run for an office. In this primary, voters were deciding who would run for mayor. At polling places around the city, New Yorkers stopped to vote on their way to work.

By 8:45 A.M., many people employed within the World Trade Center were already at work. Men and women were at their desks in hundreds of business offices. Others were cooking and serving food in restaurants and snack bars. Some were maintaining the buildings' electrical and plumbing systems. In the World Trade Center's shopping mall, clerks were opening retail stores for the day.

Nestor Zwyhun, a businessman, was just arriving. Zwyhun was walking up the block toward the World Trade

Center when suddenly he heard a sound "like a jet engine at full throttle." Zwyhun looked up at the sky. A plane was streaking toward the Center's Twin Towers. The jet plunged into North Tower. Flames shot out through shattered windows. Billows of smoke followed. Glass, concrete, and chunks of metal from the building and plane rained down on the sidewalks and streets below. "I stood there for two seconds, then ran," Zwyhun said.[2]

Construction foreman Rob Marchesano was working at a site near the World Trade Center. He was startled by the sound of a roar overhead. He looked up and saw the jet flying fast and low—so low that Marchesano feared it would hit his crane. Then, as the plane approached North Tower, he noticed that it appeared to tilt at the last second, almost as if the pilot wanted the wings to hit as many floors as possible.[3]

The speeding jet struck the 110-story tower around floor 102. The explosion upon impact was like a bomb.

Cantor Fitzgerald, a financial services company, had offices on several upper floors of North Tower. On the 103rd floor, a conference call by speaker phone was taking place with the firm's Los Angeles office. Those listening in Los Angeles heard the explosion through the phone. They asked what was happening. "I think a plane just hit us," someone in New York responded. For five minutes, the people in Los Angeles listened helplessly as their colleagues cried out, "Somebody's got to help us. . . . We can't get out. . . . The place is filling with smoke." Then the phone went dead.[4]

Timothy Snyder was working in his 85th floor office in North Tower when the first plane crashed several floors above him. He heard a very loud "slamming" sound and felt the building sway. Unsure if the building would remain standing, he held on to his desk. Outside his window, he could see debris falling. After several seconds,

*P*eople run through dust and debris that fills the air like falling snow in the aftermath of a jet crashing into one of the Twin Towers of the World Trade Center on the morning of September 11, 2001.

the building stopped moving. He knew he had to get out, quickly.[5]

Insurance broker James Cutler was in the Akbar restaurant on the ground floor of the World Trade Center when he heard three loud "booms." Smoke blew open the kitchen doors and the ceiling suddenly caved in. Bodies were everywhere. "It was mayhem," Cutler recalled.[6]

Hursley Lever, a mechanic, was working in the basement of the North Tower when the plane hit. At first, Lever thought a transformer had blown. "Then I walk toward the door and heard a big explosion," he said. "And when I look, I see a ball of fire coming toward the door."

Lever was flung across the room by the blast. The lights went out and black smoke engulfed the room. A coworker called out to Lever, asking him if he was okay. Lever said he was, but that he could not walk. Lever told his coworker to "stay low" and "stay behind me." Lever crawled toward a door and hoped it was not locked.[7]

Fire and debris were falling from the upper levels of the tower to the ground. Smoke poured from all four sides of the tower.

People began to flood the building's emergency staircases to escape. As they fled North Tower, they were all confused, frightened, and unsure. What could have caused this? Could it have been a terrible accident? Or was it the result of something more sinister?

CHAPTER 2

The Towers and Terrorism

"**I**ncidentally, if you're going to build a great project," wrote public relations expert Lee K. Jaffe, "you should build the world's tallest building."[1]

Jaffe's memo was sent in 1960 to a committee that was studying the possibility of building a great project. The Port Authority of New York and New Jersey, a two-state government agency, was considering building an enormous new office complex in New York City. The complex would house all kinds of businesses involved in world trade. Importers, exporters, shipping companies, and international investment companies could all be located there.

From the beginning, the World Trade Center was planned to be very important. It would stand on a fourteen-acre site at the southern end of Manhattan. The complex would look out over New York Harbor, the Statue of Liberty, and New Jersey.

Minoru Yamasaki, a Japanese-American architect, was

hired to design the project. He was told the buildings needed to contain 12 million square feet of floor space and that they had to fit on a fourteen acre site. Yamasaki had nearly a hundred different ideas for the project. Finally, he chose a plan with two tall towers, each 110 stories tall, with an open plaza and several lower buildings at their base.[2]

More than 50,000 people would work at the World Trade Center. In addition, approximately 100,000 business visitors and tourists were expected there each day. Besides offices, the World Trade Center would have stores, restaurants, snack bars, a hotel, police station, and

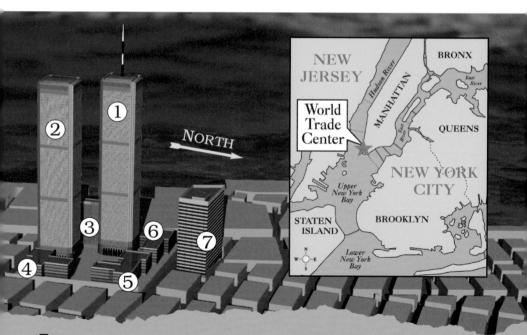

Among the seven main buildings that made up the World Trade Center were North Tower (1 World Trade Center), South Tower (2 World Trade Center), and the Marriott Hotel (3 World Trade Center). The inset map shows the five boroughs that comprise New York City: Manhattan, the Bronx, Queens, Brooklyn, and Staten Island.

galleries for exhibitions. Under the complex, parking garages and subway tunnels would accommodate the daily flow of traffic. A quarter of a mile up, visitors could enjoy spectacular forty-five-mile views. The highest open air observation deck in the world would sit atop South Tower.

In 1972, the 1,368 foot-tall North Tower was completed. South Tower, at 1,362 feet, followed in 1973. They were the two tallest buildings in the world—for about a year. In 1974, the Sears Tower in Chicago surpassed them by eighty-six feet.

The Twin Towers of the World Trade Center quickly became a symbol of trade and commerce in the United States. Certain buildings around the world are seen as symbols of their country, such as the Eiffel Tower in France, the Taj Mahal in India, and the Parthenon in Greece. Being seen as a symbol of the U.S. also made the World Trade Center a potential target, however. Those who resented U.S. power and influence might attack America by striking at the Twin Towers.

On Friday, February 26, 1993, a yellow rental van drove into the underground garage of the World Trade Center. A 1,200-pound homemade bomb was concealed inside the van. The driver parked and departed. Just after noon, the bomb exploded. The explosion smashed cars and trucks, crumbled concrete, and damaged steel columns that held up North Tower. It blasted out a crater nearly 150 feet in diameter and more than five stories deep.

Six people were killed and at least a thousand others were injured.

When the bomb exploded, more than 50,000 people were evacuated from the World Trade Center. Many escaped in darkness because the bomb had cut electrical lines. There were no lights in some emergency staircases.

Six men were arrested and charged for conspiring to bomb the World Trade Center. They were tried in United States courts and found guilty of multiple crimes, including murder. Each one was sentenced to at least 240 years in jail to ensure that none of them would ever be released.

The 1993 bombing of the World Trade Center was a terrorist attack. At the time, it was one of the deadliest acts of terrorism ever to occur in the United States. Terrorism is the systematic spread of fear (usually through violence) as a means toward attaining a goal (usually a political goal).

Ramzi Yousef, a self-proclaimed Muslim fundamentalist, was the mastermind of the plot. At his sentencing, Yousef made a long statement in the courthouse, denouncing the U.S. government as "liars and butchers" for its support of Israel. "Yes, I am a terrorist," he said, "and proud of it as long as it is against the U.S. government."[3]

The goals of terrorists are often unclear. Some terrorist acts are intended as revenge—the terrorists strike out because they believe their country or religion or society has been mistreated. Sometimes terrorist groups issue demands. For example, terrorists may demand that certain prisoners be released. Other terrorists aim to disrupt a society or government by simply killing as many people as possible. Sometimes, fear itself is their goal.

After the 1993 bombing, the World Trade Center was repaired and reopened. Many businesses there made new emergency plans. They outlined procedures for their employees to follow—which staircases to use, where to find first aid supplies and fire extinguishers, and where to meet after evacuating the building. Some companies supplied employees with survival packs. Mizuho Bank, for example, gave its workers packs containing a flashlight, glow stick, and a hood to slip over the head to make breathing easier in case of smoke.[4]

Many people in the World Trade Center on the morning of September 11, 2001, had worked there during the 1993 bombing. They knew that in a crisis it was important not to panic. After the jet struck North Tower and the alarms sounded, men and women began to exit the building in a quick but orderly fashion. The stairwells were packed, but people assisted each other. They helped burn victims and other injured people.

Barbara Chandler worked on the 77th floor of North Tower. After the plane struck, her office suite began to fill with smoke. She was one of many who escaped through the stairwells. "People were amazing," she recalled, "taking care of each other, passing water out, taking care of our pregnant colleagues."[5]

In one case, a blind man, Mike Hingson, was assisted in his escape from the 78th floor of North Tower by his guide dog, Roselle. It was hot in the stairwells and the smell of jet fuel was very strong. People passed along water bottles to Hingson so that both he and the dog could drink.[6]

Meanwhile, many of the people in South Tower were unsure what to do. Official announcements instructed them to remain where they were. The threat was limited to North Tower, the announcements proclaimed—South Tower was safe. Some decided to stay; others left. As people began to make their way down the stairwells, they were met by officials with bullhorns. These officials told

*M*ike Hingson and his guide dog, Roselle, had to escape the 78th floor of North Tower after a plane crashed into the building on the morning of September 11, 2001.

them that it was safer within the tower than it was outside. Again, many ignored the warnings and pressed on. A few turned around and returned to their offices.[7]

New York City Mayor Rudolph Giuliani had been at a private breakfast meeting in midtown Manhattan when he heard about the crash. Immediately, he left to meet Deputy Mayor Joseph J. Lhota at the World Trade Center. After arriving on the scene, the mayor and his aides began

*A*n injured woman is assisted by Deputy U.S. Marshal Dominic Guadagnoli in the wake of the plane crash at the World Trade Center on the morning of September 11, 2001.

to search for working phone lines, because their cell phones were no longer working due to the disruption of transmitters atop the World Trade Center. They entered an office building just north of the towers, where they set up a temporary command post. There, the mayor's chief of staff, Anthony Carbonetti, briefly spoke with President George W. Bush. The president was in Sarasota, Florida, where he had been scheduled to speak at an elementary school.[8]

As people evacuated the towers, emergency help was almost instantly on the way. New York City firemen, policemen, and medical personnel were racing to the scene. Some policemen were already there because they had an office in the World Trade Center. All the major television networks aimed cameras at the Twin Towers and interrupted their regular programs to broadcast the unexplained disaster.

CHAPTER 3

"He's Not Going to Land"

Shortly before the plane crash at North Tower, the Federal Aviation Administration (FAA) notified military authorities of two planes hijacked out of Boston's Logan Airport. About ten minutes later, after North Tower had been struck, two U.S. fighter jets took off from Otis Air Force base in Massachusetts. Their orders were to fly toward New York City.[1]

As people continued to stream down the stairwells of North Tower, the smell of burning jet fuel became overwhelming. Some covered their mouths with their shirts, their ties—anything to help them breathe more easily. Word began to spread among them that a 767 jet had hit the building. Many assumed this was a tragic accident.

Even with his injured leg, Hursley Lever managed to lead himself and a coworker from the basement of the North Tower to the ground floor. Lever later credited his Army combat training with helping him make it out alive. When the two men emerged, a policeman shouted to them to stay down. Lever and his coworker reached a nearby vehicle—a Secret Service car. (The Secret Service,

the government agency that protects the president and other important government officials, also had offices in the World Trade Center.) Lever heard an incredible message come over the vehicle's two-way radio: A second jet was headed toward the World Trade Center.[2]

By 9:00 A.M., air traffic controllers on Long Island had caught sight of this second jet as it entered city airspace. At this point, they were still looking for American Flight 11 out of Boston. They knew that it had been hijacked, but did not know it was the plane that had struck North Tower. Now, as this second plane approached, they were unsure if it was also hijacked or if it was just a distressed craft trying to land at a local airport. As it began its descent toward the World Trade Center, one of the controllers suddenly stood up. "He's not going to land," he said. "He's going in."[3]

By this time, nearly every cable, network, and local television station had cameras locked on to the Twin Towers of the World Trade Center. Millions of Americans were now seeing the events in New York as they were unfolding. Live images of North Tower were broadcast as smoke engulfed its upper floors. Thousands of people on the streets in New York City were staring at the building in disbelief. At 9:03 A.M., they watched helplessly as the second jet pierced the upper floors of South Tower. A monstrous ball of orange fire erupted on impact.

The second plane is seen just before it collides with South Tower on the morning of September 11, 2001.

With his injured leg, Hursley Lever was powerless to do anything but watch it all happen. "I hear *boom*," Lever said. "And when I look, I see people jumping out of the building, one after the other, the building on fire. . . . [And] I can't run. I can't go anywhere."[4]

Twenty-one-year-old student Joshua Fifer lived just a few blocks away from the World Trade Center. He was forced to evacuate his apartment so quickly that he did not even have time to put on shoes. "I saw at least seven people jumping [from the Towers]," he recalled. "You can see a person going straight down, no floating or anything. It's the sickest thing you've ever seen in your whole life."[5] One man and woman held hands as they leapt from the building together.[6]

When the first jet struck North Tower, many people thought that the disaster was a horrible accident. Eighteen minutes later, when the second plane hit South Tower, it was clear that this was a planned and deadly attack.

CHAPTER 4

War Zone

Shortly after the second tower was struck, President Bush made a brief statement to the press in Florida. "Ladies and Gentlemen," he said, "This is a difficult moment for America." He explained, "Today we've had a national tragedy. Two airplanes have crashed into the World Trade Center in an apparent terrorist attack on our country."[1] After addressing the press, President Bush was hurried off to Air Force One, the president's official plane, and departed Florida. Air Force fighter jets flew nearby, ready to protect the president.

Back in Washington, D.C., people were nervous. Along with the rest of the country, they knew of the events at the World Trade Center. Many people who worked nearby at the Pentagon were apprehensive. As the head-quarters of the government's military operations, the Pentagon also seemed a prime target for a terrorist attack.

The Pentagon is the home of the U.S. Department of Defense. The United States Navy, Air Force, and

*A*n aerial photo of the Pentagon taken in 1975.

Army are all based there. The enormous five-sided building is located just across the Potomac River from Washington, D.C. It is one of the largest office buildings in the world and covers twenty-nine acres. Approximately 24,000 people, military personnel and civilians, work there. The groundbreaking ceremony for the Pentagon was held on September 11, 1941, and the building opened fifteen months later.

Former Marine Mike Slater was one of the many people working in the Pentagon on the morning of September 11, 2001. After the attacks on the World Trade Center, he made a prediction to his coworkers: "We're next," he said.[2]

American Airlines Flight 77 had departed Dulles Airport outside of Washington, D.C., at 8:10 A.M. Among the passengers was television commentator Barbara Olson. At 9:25 A.M., Olson used her cell phone to call her husband, U.S. Solicitor General Theodore Olson, a high-ranking Justice Department official. "Can you believe this?" she said. "We're being hijacked." Olson's call was cut off, but she dialed her husband right back. When she did, Theodore Olson told her about the events at the World Trade Center. Barbara Olson said that she, her fellow passengers, and the flight crew had been herded into the back of the plane by hijackers armed with knives. Olson's last words to her husband were, "What do I tell the pilot to do?"[3]

In the Pentagon, it was about 9:40 A.M. when Mike Slater heard a sound "like a roar. I knew it was a bomb or something."[4] American Flight 77 slammed into the west side of the Pentagon. The impact was so powerful it knocked people out of their chairs and off their feet. David Theall worked in a first-floor office. He was on the phone when the plane struck the building. He was thrown through a wall that "just gave way—the walls just crumpled up like pieces of paper." The phone was still in his hand.[5]

Theall and a coworker crawled through the rubble of the collapsed ceiling that had fallen on top of them. "I started seeing Army faces," Theall said, "but everyone was this eerie white [color from the dust]." The two managed to get safely outdoors. Over the next several hours, they assisted in the evacuation of the Pentagon. They loaded burn victims into helicopters and helped nurses provide emergency care.[6]

It was Sheila Moody's first day on the job as an accountant at the Pentagon. Inside her first-floor office, she heard a whooshing sound. She felt a gust of wind and wondered where it could be coming from. Then there was a burst of flames. Moody looked down and saw her hands had caught fire. She shook them violently, putting out the flames. Smoke was everywhere. She heard a man's voice call out to her, followed by the flush of a fire extinguisher. Then the man reached out to her and helped her escape.[7]

Mark Thaggard, an office manager in the Pentagon,

S moke and flames fill the air outside of the Pentagon after a plane crashed into the building on the morning of September 11, 2001.

was there when the plane hit. "It was chaotic. It was unbelievable. . . . We could not believe this was happening." Another civilian Pentagon worker recalled, "We heard a loud blast, and I felt a gust of wind. I heard a loud explosion and somebody said, 'Run, let's get out of here.' And I ran."[8]

Mere minutes before the crash at the Pentagon, two fighter jets from Langley Air Force Base in Virginia had taken off to defend the skies over Washington. By radio, the Langley fighter jet leader was asked, "Can you confirm that the Pentagon is on fire?" The pilots could see smoke. They confirmed the report. Then they received their next order: A command to "protect the White House at all costs."[9]

Then the fighter pilots heard an order that had never been issued before. All non-military aircraft were ordered to land. More than 4,000 planes were in the skies. Most flights arriving from other countries were diverted to Canada. For the first time in U.S. history, the airways were closed. The government was determined to stop any more attacks.

In Washington, the White House was quickly evacuated. The Capitol, the Supreme Court, and all other federal buildings were closed shortly afterward. Vice President Dick Cheney and Laura Bush, the President's wife, were rushed into a secure bunker near the White House.

Back in New York, some safety improvements made at the World Trade Center after the 1993 bombing helped make the evacuation easier. Backup electrical lines kept lights on in many stairwells.[10] Still, lower-level stairwells

Fireman Mike Kehoe assists in the evacuation of North Tower on September 11. Kehoe was later able to escape the building uninjured.

were flooded with water from burst pipes and building sprinkler systems. Steadily, those who could continued down and out of the towers. Policemen and fireman went up the stairs to rescue others.

Already, scores of people were dead. All the crew, passengers, and hijackers on the planes had died. Those on the floors that were directly hit had perished. Many were still leaping to their deaths to escape the flames. On the ground, people were injured and killed by glass, concrete, and steel crashing down from the building's heights.

Then, at 10:00 A.M., a horrible rumbling came from South Tower. Smoke and dust spewed from the top of the building. Black streaks shot out like streamers. It looked almost like fireworks in reverse—a deadly dark blast against the sparkling blue sky.

"My God, it's falling," someone shouted.[11] In front of thousands of witnesses and millions of television viewers, South Tower crumbled to the ground.

The burning jet fuel had weakened the tower's steel support structure. The towers had originally been designed to withstand the impact of a plane. But these jets carried enough fuel to sustain cross-country flights—more than 60,000 pounds of fuel per plane. On impact, the tanks exploded. The massive load of fuel fed the flames. The fire was not hot enough to melt steel, but it was hot enough to soften it. Once the steel support was sufficiently weakened, South Tower gave way.[12]

Floor after floor slammed down. As each one fell, it

The top of South Tower appears to erupt, almost like a volcano, as it suddenly collapses shortly after being crashed into by a 767 jet.

crushed everything in the space just below it. Computers, desks, file cabinets, chairs lights, potted plants, washrooms, and mementos on desks were all flattened. Men and women on the floors were killed as the building collapsed. A ferocious wind, thick with smoke and concrete dust, blasted out of the falling tower. It knocked over vans, threw people from their feet, and tore walls off of buildings. Smoke and dust burned people's eyes.

Mike Panone worked in a bank across the street from the World Trade Center. As South Tower began to collapse, he tried to run. "The sky was just a big, black cloud," he said, "and I couldn't outrun the cloud."[13]

Inside the building where Mayor Giuliani and his aides were located, they heard the rumbling. No one inside knew what was happening. The room filled with dust as the front of the building began to crumble. A security guard led the mayor and his team to the basement, where they escaped through a maze of underground tunnels.

The rumbling finally stopped. Outside, survivors were stunned by the sight. Soot, ash, and concrete dust

*P*edestrians run for cover as one of the Twin Towers of the World Trade Center collapses on September 11, 2001.

were a foot deep. It looked like dense, gray snow. In the air, millions of sheets of paper fluttered down from desks and offices that no longer existed.

Even after South Tower collapsed, rescue personnel were still trying to get people out of North Tower. They knew that the second tower would probably collapse soon also, but they courageously pressed on. They were determined to save as many lives as possible.

Jim Pesomen had escaped from the 81st floor of North Tower. "The toughest part was watching the firemen go back in the building as it was coming down," Pesomen said. "Those guys, they have courage, knowing what they know."[14]

At 10:29 A.M., the rumbling started again, like the return of a horrible nightmare. People closest to the building said that it sounded like snapping spaghetti as the steel tubes that held up the building broke.[15] As it fell, North Tower was like an erupting volcano. Smoke and concrete spewed forth. Dust and debris blasted down the narrow streets.

It had taken Mike Hingson and his guide dog, Roselle, a half hour to complete their journey down the stairwells of North Tower to safety. When he got outside, he was covered in dust. "I could feel it in my lungs," he said. "I coughed it up." Although he could not see North Tower collapse, he could still hear it and feel it, vividly. "It was like a train coming straight at you. You knew it was a building, you just didn't know which way it was going."[16]

Forty-six-year-old volunteer fireman Mike Athemas

People make their way through the ash and debris in the aftermath of the collapse of the Twin Towers.

remembered, "Everywhere you turned, there was someone taking bodies out of the rubble." Craig Gutkes, another fireman, recalled, "It was like a war zone when we got there. There were body parts all over the street."[17]

Taxi driver Amir Chaudhary watched from across the Hudson River in Jersey City, New Jersey, as the second tower collapsed. "In the blink of my eye, the Twin Towers were gone," he said. "There was no boom even. Didn't hear anything. Guys were on their knees crying, begging me to give them a ride away. I feel like maybe it's a bad dream: If I wake up, I could get the Twin Towers back."[18]

For almost thirty years, the towers stood over a quarter of a mile tall. In one hour and thirty-six minutes, they were reduced to a vast heap of burning rubble.

CHAPTER 5

Heroes

eremy Glick always had a fondness for comic-book heroes. On Labor Day, September 3, 2001, Glick celebrated his thirty-first birthday. He spent part of the day on a boat with friends—all of them dressed up as superheroes. Two friends dressed as Batman, while another dressed as Superman. Glick wore a green felt mask like Green Lantern.[1]

Eight days later, Jeremy Glick became a real-life hero.

Glick had boarded United Airlines Flight 93 in Newark, New Jersey, shortly before 8:00 A.M. on September 11, 2001. The flight was bound for San Francisco. Around 9:45, Glick used his mobile phone to call his wife, Lyzbeth, back in New Jersey. She was staying with her parents while he was out of town. He told her that his plane had been hijacked by three Middle Eastern men in red headbands. The men carried knives and claimed to have a bomb. Other passengers who made calls on cell phones had told him that two planes had crashed into the Twin Towers. Glick asked his wife if this was true. Yes, she told him, it was true.

At this point, Glick told his wife that he and several other passengers were considering "jumping" the hijackers. Glick wished his wife a happy life and told her to take care of their three-month-old daughter. Lyzbeth Glick became too upset to continue talking. She handed the phone to her father, Richard Makely. Then she picked up her baby daughter and held her. Through the phone, Makely heard screams, followed by a brief silence. Then he heard more screams before the line went dead.[2]

In Shanksville, Pennsylvania, Kelly Leverknight was watching the news in her home. She heard the roar of a jet low overhead. "It was headed toward the school," she said, referring to Shanksville-Stonycreek Elementary School. The school held 501 students, including Leverknight's three children.[3]

Seconds later, at about 10:06 A.M., Flight 93 crashed into an empty field, two miles short of the school. "I just keep thinking—two miles," Principal Rosemarie Tipton said. "There but for the grace of God—two miles."[4] Everyone aboard the plane perished, but no one on the ground was killed.

At least three other men are also believed to have participated with Jeremy Glick in resisting the terrorists aboard Flight 93: Tom Burnett, Mark Bingham, and Todd Beamer.

Todd Beamer had used an airplane phone to contact GTE Airfone operator Lisa Jefferson. He said that a group

*T*he crash site of United Airlines Flight 93, just outside Shanksville, Pennsylvania.

of men aboard the plane were planning to resist the hijackers. "We're going to do something," Beamer told Jefferson. "I know I'm not going to get out of this." Beamer asked Jefferson to pray with him. Then he asked her to call his wife and children to let them know he loved them. Beamer dropped the phone, but the line remained open.

"Let's roll," Jefferson heard Beamer say. Jefferson then heard several minutes of chaos before the connection was lost.[5]

"That was Todd," Beamer's wife, Lisa, later said. "My two boys even say 'let's roll.' My little one says 'come on Mom, let's roll.' That's something they picked up from their Dad."[6]

As rescue workers rushed to the site of the crashed jet in Pennsylvania, the crises continued in Washington and New York. At the Pentagon, firefighters were attacking the blaze. They worked to keep the fire from spreading to other parts of the building. Evacuation and rescues were continuing. Around Washington, D.C., federal buildings were closing. Streets were packed with cars as commuters and visitors left. In New York City, firemen and other rescue workers were still trying to recover as many hurt and injured people as possible from the wreckage of the Twin Towers.

The Reverend Mychal Judge had been a New York City Fire Department chaplain since 1982. Known as Father

Lisa Beamer holds her younger son, Andrew, in her lap while her eldest son, David, admires a photo of his Dad, Todd Beamer. Todd Beamer is one of several passengers aboard Flight 93 believed to have resisted their hijackers.

Mike, he was a beloved figure in the department. When he had heard of the first plane crash that morning, Father Mike got two firemen to drive him downtown right away. Shortly after arriving, the priest came across a fireman who had been struck dead by a falling body. Father Mike immediately ran over to administer last rites. As he removed his white helmet, he was struck in the head and killed by falling debris.

Firefighters carried their beloved chaplain to nearby St. Peter's church. There, they laid him before the altar. They covered Father Mike with a white cloth and his priest's stole. They placed his helmet and his badge on his chest.[7]

Doctors, nurses, medical technicians, lifeguards, construction workers, and passersby all rushed to help those in need. People with medical training performed triage— a process of sorting injured people into groups based on their immediate needs and likely benefit from treatment. Victims were color-coded by their degree of injury so the medical teams could respond most effectively. People with minor injuries, called the walking wounded, were given green cards. Victims with serious, but not life-threatening injuries were labeled yellow. Those with immediately life-threatening conditions were labeled red. Finally, black tags were for the dead.[8]

As rescue workers continued to pour into the city, thousands of civilians crossed the bridges over the East River out of Manhattan. This mass pilgrimage was an amazing sight. "Just a sea of heads all moving in the same direction, away from Manhattan," Mike Vani observed from the middle of the Manhattan Bridge.[9]

The Brooklyn Bridge was also flooded with people. The large crowd remained mostly calm as they crossed. Some wore dust masks, while some others held wet paper towels over their faces. Once they made it across to Brooklyn, many of the people broke down and wept. Some tried in vain to use their cell phones to contact loved ones to let them know they were alright. Others formed long lines in front of pay phones.[10]

Ambulances kept streaming in and out of city hospitals.

*T*housands flood the Brooklyn Bridge on a mass pilgrimage out of Manhattan on the morning of September 11, 2001.

The doctors and nurses at St. Vincent's Hospital in Greenwich Village were running out of medicine for burn victims. Some on the hospital staff were sent out to local drug stores to buy more. One staff member went out with a grocery cart that had a sign attached, reading, "WE NEED CLOTHING DONATIONS." Within the hour, neighborhood residents brought dozens of bags full of clothing for victims whose clothes had been burned off.[11]

At blood centers around the city, thousands of donors lined up to give blood. They wanted to make sure there would be enough blood available for the injured victims. At some centers, lines stretched around the block, while people patiently waited their turn.

As dust still fluttered down from above, Mayor Giuliani was out in the ash- and soot-covered streets. He pulled off his gas mask and urged survivors to go north to safety. Immediately, he met with officials to learn what the rescue workers needed. He ordered the evacuation of the lower end of Manhattan—for safety and to make it easier for emergency workers to get in to do their jobs. The city's tunnels, bridges, and subways were closed, in case more attacks were planned. The primaries were postponed to a later date.

Around the country, prominent buildings and landmarks closed. In Chicago, the Sears Tower was evacuated. Disney World shut down for the day. The Hoover Dam, Mount Rushmore, and the Mall of America all closed their doors.

At 5:25 P.M., 7 World Trade Center was the third building

President Bush addresses the nation from the White House on the evening of September 11, 2001.

to collapse. All that remained of the Twin Towers was 1.5 million tons of smoldering debris.

Later in the evening, less than twelve hours after the first plane had struck the World Trade Center, President George W. Bush addressed the country from the White House in Washington, D.C.

"Today," he said, "our fellow citizens, our way of life, our very freedom came under attack in a series of deliberate and deadly terrorist acts." He spoke about the events and victims of the day. "Today our nation saw evil, the very worst of human nature. And we responded with the best of America." The president talked about rescue workers and how Americans came together to help each other. "The search is under way for those who are behind these evil acts. I have directed the full resources of our intelligence and law enforcement communities to find those responsible and bring them to justice."[12]

CHAPTER 6

"More Than Any of Us Can Bear"

In the wake of the terrorist attacks of September 11, countries from around the world sent condolences to the United States. Presidents and prime ministers expressed their outrage at the terrorists and voiced their support for the United States.

President Vladimir Putin of Russia sent a telegram to President Bush saying "Such an inhuman act should not go unpunished. The entire international community should unite in the struggle against terrorism." German Chancellor Gerhard Schroder said the attacks were "a declaration of war against the entire civilized world."[1] Tony Blair, the prime minister of Britain, condemned the terrorist attacks and promised that his country would stand "full square alongside the U.S."[2]

The United States is a member of the North Atlantic Treaty Organization (NATO). This organization was established in 1949 to provide leadership for the common defense of its member nations. It was originally founded in order to protect countries in Western Europe from the Soviet Union. After the terrorist attacks of September 11, NATO officials issued a statement: "If it is determined that this attack was directed from abroad against the United States, it shall be regarded as an action covered by Article 5 of the Washington Treaty." This Article states that any attack against a member of NATO would be considered as an attack against every member nation. This was the first time in history that this article of mutual defense was invoked and it was passed unanimously.[3] Many countries were willing to support the United States with soldiers, weapons, and diplomacy.

Ash and rubble fill the streets of lower Manhattan in the aftermath of the terrorist attacks that resulted in the destruction of the Twin Towers.

September 11 reminded many people of Pearl Harbor. On December 7, 1941, the United States Naval Base in Pearl Harbor, Hawaii, was bombed by 360 Japanese war planes. The surprise attack killed 2,403 people—mostly American sailors. As a result of this attack, the United States entered World War II the following day. At Pearl Harbor, everybody knew who was attacking. The Japanese planes were clearly marked with their country's insignia of the rising sun. On September 11, 2001, the United States did not know for certain who their attackers were.

Investigators and intelligence agencies searched for answers as rescue workers searched for survivors at the Pentagon and at the World Trade Center. At the crash site of Flight 175 in Pennsylvania there were no survivors. Investigators there were retrieving bodies and looking for clues.

At the Pentagon, firefighters dug a trench to keep the fire from spreading to other parts of the building. On Wednesday, September 12, the fire there was declared to be under control. Nearby, a temporary morgue was set up for bodies. Officials and families still hoped they might find survivors sheltered in the rubble.

The site of the World Trade Center was being called Ground Zero. This is a term normally used to describe the point on the ground below an explosion. Rescue efforts were intense, even as fires burned in the wreckage. These fires would continue to smolder for months. "You keep hitting it again and again with water," firefighter Jose Maldonado remarked in late November 2001. "But the fire

This aerial photo taken on September 14, 2001, shows the incredible damage caused to the west face of the Pentagon three days earlier by a crashing jet.

won't give up. It is just a constant fight." Firefighting experts were calling it the longest commercial building fire in U.S. history.[4]

Canine rescue teams played an important role in recovering victims at Ground Zero. In the hours immediately following the building collapses, search dogs sniffed out six people still alive in the rubble. As the days passed, these animals and their human counterparts worked sixteen-hour shifts in an effort to save lives.[5] Pet supply companies sent padded dog boots to New York to help protect the dogs' paws from the burning debris and broken glass at Ground Zero.

Sgt. John McLoughlin, a Port Authority policeman, was one of the lucky survivors. He was rescued from the rubble the morning after the attacks. He had been buried under forty feet of debris. Both his legs were broken. Rescue workers heard faint sounds of McLoughlin struggling. They eventually got a two-way microphone into the little space where he was trapped. As they dug, they talked to him to keep his mind off his pain. When they were finally able to pull him out, the surrounding crowd cheered. "It's wonderful," Battalion Chief Gary Connelly said. "None of us can imagine how he survived. . . . [H]e is a tough dude."[6]

Days after the attack, Hursley Lever sat on a bed at Bellevue Hospital, thankful to have survived. Had he been next door in the pump room at the time the first plane hit, the rushing fireball would have killed him. Had his ankle not been broken, he may have tried to help rescue fellow coworkers and could have died when the tower collapsed. "I feel blessed that I'm alive," Lever said.[7]

Across Manhattan, photos of missing people were posted everywhere. They were pasted on walls, lampposts and parked cars. Some were

One week later, this crumpled shell is all that is left standing of one the World Trade Center's Twin Towers.

taped to trees, on the side of newsstands and benches, to phone booths and bus stops. Many of the photos posted were of mothers and fathers hugging their children; the mother or father was now missing.

A plywood partition at the First Avenue entrance of Bellevue Hospital became known as the Wall of Prayer because of all the pictures and messages posted there. In Union Square, a similar memorial was erected. Students from nearby New York University brought flowers and lit candles. Some taped up large strips of paper for people to write down their thoughts.

New York Police Detectives set up a headquarters in the Armory at Lexington Avenue and 26th Street, where they could interview people who were searching for missing loved ones. Michael Rodriguez went there after checking every hospital and morgue in search of his sister, Lisa. "I feel like I've been to the moon and back fifteen times," he said. "It's utter helplessness, that's what it feels like."[8]

Many volunteers showed up to help with rescue efforts. They brought supplies and equipment with them. Donations of clothes and food for workers and victims' families poured in. Meatpackers and restaurants sent bags of ice to help cool drinks for the rescue workers. Stores sent shopping carts full of socks to help protect workers' feet. Donated pies, granola bars, bagels, sandwiches, and potato chips were set out for snacks.

No one knew how many people were killed. It was clear, though, that thousands of families had lost

*T*he Wall of Prayer outside the entrance of Bellevue Hospital on the East Side of Manhattan, one week after the terrorist attacks.

someone. When asked how many casualties there were at the World Trade Center, Mayor Giuliani responded, "More than any of us can bear."[9]

Overall, almost 3,000 people at the World Trade Center were either reported missing or confirmed dead, with an additional 157 more having died on the two hijacked planes, including ten hijackers. At the Pentagon, 125 people were either missing or dead, with sixty-four more having died on the hijacked plane, including five hijackers. Aboard Flight 93, which crashed in Pennsylvania, forty-four died, including four hijackers.[10] Citizens of eighty different countries were killed in the attacks.

In the weeks following the attacks, individuals, companies, and organizations across the nation donated money to help the victims of the attacks and their families. Famous entertainers hosted benefits. Whoopi Goldberg, Paul Simon, Tom Cruise, and dozens of other celebrities held a television fund-raiser called "America: A Tribute to Heroes." The event raised millions of dollars. Paul McCartney, Bon Jovi, the Goo Goo Dolls, and a host of other stars performed a "Concert for New York" at Madison Square Garden. Former President Bill Clinton and former presidential candidate Bob Dole started a college scholarship fund for children of September 11 victims called "Families of Freedom." Basketball superstar Michael Jordan donated one year of his salary, a million dollars, to disaster relief. Companies including General Electric, Microsoft, and A.I.G. pledged multimillion-dollar gifts. Schools held car washes and collected coins to send to relief efforts. One four-year-old girl sent $4.37.[11]

President Bush declared Friday, September 14, 2001, a day of prayer and remembrance. American flags were flown at half-staff as a sign of respect for the victims. Candlelight vigils were held in cities and towns around the country. Around the world, other countries showed their grief and respect. In London, for the first time in history, "The Star Spangled Banner" was played for the changing of the guard at Buckingham Palace. In South Africa, firefighters in Johannesburg flew an American flag at half-staff. In France, the front page of the newspaper *Le Monde* read: "We are all Americans."

CHAPTER 7

Why?

Father Mychal Judge was buried on Saturday, September 15. His death certificate bore the number one, making him the first official casualty of the attacks. More than 2,000 mourners attended his funeral. Among them were former President Clinton, countless firefighters, and many of the AIDS patients that Father Mike had helped. Those in attendance shook with grief as the Reverend Michael Duffy gave the homily. "He loved his Fire Department," Duffy said, "and the men in it."[1]

Firemen, police, and EMTs (Emergency Medical Technicians) who died in the World Trade Center collapse and in the attack on the Pentagon were hailed as heroes. So were the passengers aboard Flight 93. Many people believed that those who resisted the terrorists aboard Flight 93 deserved to be awarded the Congressional Medal of Freedom—the highest award a U.S. civilian can receive.

The New York City Fire Department was left devastated.

September 11, 2001, marked the single greatest loss of life in department history. After six days of rescue efforts, the department reported almost 350 firemen as either missing or dead, including five of the department's senior officials. Among them were the highest-ranking uniformed officer of the Department, Chief Peter J. Ganci, Jr., along with First Deputy Commissioner William Feehan, Father Mychal Judge, and Chief Ray Downey. Downey was

A poster of the Reverend Mychal Judge stands outside Engine Company 1, Ladder Company 24 in midtown Manhattan on September 13, 2001. In addition to Father Mike, seven other men from Engine Company 1 were presumed to have died in the Twin Tower collapse.

the most decorated man in the department. He had headed search and rescue efforts at the World Trade Center bombing in 1993, as well as at the Oklahoma City bombing in 1995 and when TWA Flight 800 exploded off Long Island in 1996.

On September 16, the department promoted 168 members to offset the men who were lost in the collapse of the Twin Towers. At the ceremony, Mayor Giuliani made an emotional speech:

> "[Y]ou're all my heroes. . . .
> Countries that live under a rule
> of law agree on being a democracy and respect and care about
> human life the way the firefighters of New York care about
> human life. That's what we
> want. That's the future we
> want for our children, that's
> the future we want for the rest
> of the world."[2]

Many people felt guilty, wondering if they could have somehow helped prevent the awful events of September 11. Security supervisor Claudia Richey said she could never forget the face of the man she let pass at Logan Airport that

New York City Mayor Rudolph Giuliani addresses reporters outside St. Vincent's Hospital on September 11, 2001. Days later, the mayor delivered an emotional speech at a ceremony to promote 168 new firefighters to offset the losses suffered by the department as a result of the terrorist attacks.

fateful Tuesday morning. She was sure he had been one of the hijackers. The moment he walked past her was one that would haunt her. "If all those people could be alive," Richey said, "I would die right now."[3]

By September 13, authorities had determined the identities of all nineteen hijackers aboard the four planes. The investigation was piecing together who was involved and what the terrorists had planned.

The men were all linked to the terrorist network Al Qaeda. *Al Qaeda* is Arabic for "the Base." Al Qaeda was largely led and funded by a man named Osama bin Laden. Bin Laden was a multimillionaire fugitive from Saudi Arabia. In the 1980s, bin Laden moved to Afghanistan to help fight the forces of the Soviet Union, which had invaded the country. There, he received aid and training from U.S. agencies to help battle Soviet forces. Then, during the Gulf War in 1991, bin Laden's hatred of the U.S. took root. He saw the presence of American soldiers in Saudi Arabia at that time as a return to imperialist control of the Middle East by the West. Saudi Arabia is also where the cities of Mecca and Medina are located. These are among the holiest cities to the Islamic faith and are barred to non-Muslims.

In a statement he made in 1996, bin Laden denounced the "occupation" of the Arab Holy Land by "American crusader forces." He called the U.S. military presence in Saudi Arabia the "greatest aggression" against the Islamic world since the death of the prophet Mohammed in 632 A.D.[4]

Then bin Laden issued a "Declaration of Jihad." *Jihad* is a term used to describe a state of holy war in defense of Islam. The purpose of bin Laden's jihad was to overthrow the Saudi government and remove U.S. military forces from the region.[5]

Because of his opposition to the Gulf War, bin Laden was placed under house arrest in Saudi Arabia. Eventually, he fled the country in April 1991. Initially, he moved back to Afghanistan, but then relocated to Sudan in Africa a short time later. In 1996, the Sudanese government expelled bin Laden from the country due to political pressure from the U.S. This prompted bin Laden to

An image of Osama bin Laden taken from a television broadcast on October 7, 2001. In the broadcast, bin Laden praised God for the September 11 terrorist attacks.

return to Afghanistan once more. The Taliban, a government of Islamic extremists like bin Laden, had recently risen to power there. Under their rule, women were not allowed to appear in public unless their bodies and faces were covered. Men could be jailed if their beards were not long enough.

In 2000, a U.S. court found evidence linking Osama bin Laden to the 1998 bombing of American embassies in Kenya and Tanzania. Later, bin Laden would also be linked to the attack on the U.S. naval vessel, the *Cole*, in Yemen in 2000. There was also evidence of a financial connection between bin Laden and the organizers of the World Trade Center bombing in 1993.

Shortly after the attacks of September 11, 2001, a message to bin Laden was intercepted. The message proclaimed, "We have hit the targets."[6] Within days, U.S.

Numerous tributes were left at the entrances of New York City firehouses like the one shown below in the weeks following the terrorist attacks of September 11.

officials were certain that bin Laden and the Al Qaeda organization were responsible for the attacks that took place on September 11.

The roots of Al Qaeda can be traced back to the early 1990s in Egypt and Saudi Arabia. The group was comprised of Islamic radicals—people whose ideas and beliefs are extremely different from the traditional ideas of the Islamic faith. Many of these men turned to their radical ideas because they were disillusioned by the poverty and oppression they suffered. They were dissatisfied with their governments and blamed the United States for helping to keep these governments in power—or perhaps not doing enough to promote reforms.

The terrorists who hijacked those four planes on September 11 were religious extremists. Their interpretation of their religion is very different from that of most Muslims. As President Bush stated, "The terrorists practice a fringe form of Islamic extremism that has been rejected by Muslim scholars and the vast majority of Muslim clerics. A fringe movement that perverts the peaceful teaching of Islam. . . . The terrorists are traitors to their own faith, trying in effect to hijack Islam itself."[7]

But understanding the motives of the terrorists will probably not make it any easier for most people to accept the events of September 11. It is difficult to understand why such a tremendous loss of life should ever occur, or how any cause could ever justify it. In the final analysis, the terrorist attacks were senseless acts, committed by men whose minds had been twisted by hatred.

As a fire chaplain, Mychal Judge often had to console the families of firefighters who had given their lives to save others. Helping people understand why they lost someone they loved was never easy. "My God is a God of surprises," he would often say.[8] By this he meant that life is full of unexpected circumstances and that there is not always an explanation for why they occur. And even on a terrible day like September 11, good things can happen. Despite the actions of the terrorists, there were countless other acts of heroism and love. The heroes far outnumbered the villains that day.

At a memorial service just a year earlier, Father Mike had urged mourners to find strength in the happy memories they held of the people they had lost. "Open your

*M*issing persons flyers and assorted tributes adorn the Wall of Prayer outside Bellevue Hospital just one week after the terrorist attacks.

hearts, and let their spirit and life keep you going," he had told them. "When they look down, they see your love."[9]

In the weeks after the attacks, the U.S. demanded that the ruling Taliban government of Afghanistan turn over Osama bin Laden and any other members of Al Qaeda operating within the country. The Taliban refused. On October 7, 2001, the United States began a military campaign in Afghanistan designed to oust the Taliban from power and capture Osama bin Laden and any members of his Al Qaeda organization. By year's end, this campaign had successfully toppled the Taliban, though bin Laden remained unfound. But regardless of whether bin Laden is ever brought to justice, the war against terrorism will not end there. The struggle against terrorism is one that will be both long and difficult, with no clear, simple ending.

After the fall of the Soviet Union, the 1990s were a time of great peace and prosperity for the United States. Many Americans felt that war was no longer possible. The events of September 11 made people realize that peace could never be taken for granted again. But President Bush spoke words of assurance:

> "After all that has just passed, all the lives taken and all the possibilities and hopes that died with them, it is natural to wonder if America's future is one of fear. . . . But this country will define our times, not be defined by them. As long as the United States of America is determined and strong, this will not be an age of terror. This will be an age of liberty here and across the world."[10]

Chapter 1. September 11, 2001

1. Raphael Lewis, "Guard Recalls Suspects at Logan," *The Boston Globe*, September 16, 2001, p. A16.

2. "Nation Stands In Disbelief and Horror," *The Wall Street Journal*, September 12, 2001, p. A1.

3. David Maraniss, "September 11, 2001: Thousands' Workaday Scenario Turned Surreal," *The Washington Post*, September 16, 2001, p. A1.

4. "Nation Stands In Disbelief and Horror," p. A1.

5. Ibid., p. A12.

6. Ibid., p. A1.

7. Brian MacQuarrie, "In a Nightmare, Survivor Finds Rescue and Hope," *The Boston Globe*, September 16, 2001, p. A3.

Chapter 2. The Towers and Terrorism

1. Angus Kress Gillespie, *Twin Towers: The Life of New York City's World Trade Center* (New Brunswick, N.J.: Rutgers University Press, 1999), p. 46.

2. Paul Heyer, *Architects on Architecture: New Directions in America* (New York: Walker and Company, 1966), p. 194.

3. Peg Tyre, "'Proud Terrorist' Gets Life for Trade Center Bombing," *U.S. News Story Page, CNN interactive*, January 8, 1998, <http://www.cnn.com/US/9801/08/yousef.update/> (November 16, 2001).

4. David Maraniss, "September 11, 2001: Thousands' Workaday Scenario Turned Surreal," *The Washington Post*, September 16, 2001, p. A1.

5. Evan Thomas, "A New Date of Infamy," *Newsweek Extra Edition*, Vol. CXXXVIII, No. 12-A, pp. 26–27.

6. *Recording for the Blind & Dyslexic*, n.d., <http://www.rfbd.org/newsuccessbravos.htm> (December 11, 2001).

7. Michael Moss and Charles V. Bagli, "Instincts to Flee Competed With Instructions to Remain in Building," *The New York Times*, September 13, 2001, p. A6.

8. Jennifer Steinhauer, "Giuliani Takes Charge, and City Sees Him as the Essential Man," *The New York Times*, September 14, 2001, p. A2.

Chapter 3. "He's Not Going to Land"

1. "Timeline in Terrorist Attacks of Sept. 11, 2001," *The Washington Post*, September 12, 2001, <http://www.washingtonpost.com/wp-srv/nation/articles/timeline.html> (December 11, 2001).

2. Brian MacQuarrie, "In a Nightmare, Survivor Finds Rescue and Hope," *The Boston Globe*, September 16, 2001, p. A3.

3. David Maraniss, "September 11, 2001: Thousands' Workaday Scenario Turned Surreal," *The Washington Post*, September 16, 2001, p. A1.

4. MacQuarrie, p. A3.

5. "'I Saw Things No One Should Ever See,'" *Newsweek Extra Edition*, Vol. CXXXVIII, No. 12-A, p. 63.

6. Pete Hamill, "Evil From the Sky," *The New York Daily News*, September 16, 2001, p. 46.

Chapter 4. War Zone

1. George W. Bush, "Remarks by the President After Two Planes Crash Into World Trade Center," *White House News Archive*, September 11, 2001, <http://www.whitehouse.gov/news/releases/2001/09/20010911.html> (December 10, 2001).

2. Don Van Natta and Lizette Alvarez, "A Hijacked Boeing 757 Slams Into the Pentagon, Halting the Government," *The New York Times*, September 12, 2001, p. A5.

3. David Maraniss, "September 11, 2001: Thousands' Workaday Scenario Turned Surreal," *The Washington Post*, September 16, 2001, p. A1.

4. Van Natta and Alvarez, p. A5.

5. Susanne M. Schafer, "Pentagon Explosion Stuns Survivors," *The Washington Post*, September 12, 2001, <http://www.washingtonpost.com/wp-dyn/articles/A20834-2001Sep12.html> (September 16, 2001).

6. Ibid.

7. Maraniss, p. A1.

8. "Nation Stands In Disbelief and Horror," *The Wall Street Journal*, September 12, 2001, p. A12.

9. Matthew L. Wald with Kevin Sack, "'We Have Some Planes,' Hijackers Said on Sept. 11," *The New York Times*, October 16, 2001, p. A1.

10. Michael Moss and Charles V. Bagli, "Instincts to Flee Competed With Instructions to Remain in Building," *The New York Times*, September 13, 2001, p. A6.

11. "Nation Stands In Disbelief and Horror," p. A12.

12. James Glanz, "Towers Believed to be Safe Proved Vulnerable to an Intense Jet Fuel Fire, Experts Say," *The New York Times*, September 12, 2001, p.A3.

13. Somini Sangupta, "A Battered Retreat On Bridges To the East," *The New York Times*, September 12, 2001, p. A11.

14. Evan Thomas, "A New Date of Infamy," *Newsweek Extra Edition*, Vol. CXXXVIII, No. 12-A, p. 27.

15. "September 11, 2001," *Radified*, n.d., <http://radified.com/911/911_collapse.htm> (December 11, 2001).

16. "Guide Dog Leads Blind Man to Safety from Tower Attack," *N.J. News*, September 20, 2001, <http://www.northjersey.com/news/3wtcdog20200109201.htm> (December 3, 2001).

17. "Nation Stands In Disbelief and Horror," p. A12.

18. Ibid.

Chapter 5. Heroes

1. Jodi Wilgoren, "Farewell Image of a Friend: Fighting Back," *The New York Times*, September 17, 2001, p. A11.

2. Evan Thomas, "A New Date of Infamy," *Newsweek Extra Edition*, Vol. CXXXVIII, No. 12-A, p. 22.

3. Nancy Gibbs, "If You Want To Humble an Empire," *Time*, September 11, 2001, p. 40.

4. Ibid.

5. Charles Lane, Don Phillips and David Snyder, "A Sky Filled With Chaos, Uncertainty and True Heroism," *The Washington Post*, September 17, 2001, p. A3.

6. Jim McKinnon, "The Phone Line From Flight 93 Was Still Open When a GTE Operator Heard Todd Beamer Say: 'Are You Guys Ready? Let's Roll,'" *Pittsburgh Post-Gazette*, September 16, 2001, p. A1.

7. Michael Daly, "His Words Still Heal Us," *The New York Daily News*, September 16, 2001, p. 18.

8. Nancy Gibbs, p. 43.

9. Somini Sangupta, "A Battered Retreat On Bridges To the East," *The New York Times*, September 12, 2001, p. A11.

10. Ibid.

11. Nancy Gibbs, p. 44.

12. George W. Bush, "Bush's Remarks to the Nation on the Terrorist Attacks," *The New York Times*, September 12, 2001, p. A4.

Chapter 6. "More Than Any of Us Can Bear"

1. Steven Erlanger, "European Nations Stand with U.S., Ready to Respond," *The New York Times*, September 12, 2001, p. A23.

2. "Reaction From Around the World," *The New York Times*, September 12, 2001, p. A23.

3. Suzanne Daley, "For First Time, NATO Invokes Joint Defense Pact With U.S.," *The New York Times*, September 13, 2001, p. A17.

4. Eric Lipton and Andrew C. Revkin, "With Water and Sweat, Fighting the Most Stubborn Fire," *The New York Times*, November 19, 2001, p. B1.

5. Alex Lieber, "Heroes of the World Trade Center," *PetPlace.com*, n.d., <http://www.petplace.com/Articles/artShow.asp?artID=4081> (September 23, 2001).

6. Dexter Filkins, "Entombed for a Day, Then Found," *The New York Times*, September 13, 2001, p. A9.

7. Brian MacQuarrie, "In a Nightmare, Survivor Finds Rescue and Hope," *The Boston Globe*, September 16, 2001, p. A3.

8. Corky Siemaszko, "Kin Create Vast Gallery of Untold Still Missing," *The New York Daily News*, September 14, 2001, p. 31.

9. Pete Hamill, "Evil From the Sky," *The New York Daily News*, September 16, 2001, p. 51.

10. "Dead and Missing," *The New York Times*, December 11, 2001, p. B2.

11. Elissa Gootman, "A Range of Donors Help Those in the Rescue Effort," *The New York Times*, September 14, 2001, p. A8.

Chapter 7. Why?

1. Patrice O'Shaughnessy, "Fire Chaplain Is Laid to Rest," *The New York Daily News*, September 16, 2001, p. 19.

2. Rudolph Giuliani, "The Mayor's Remarks: 'You're All My Heroes,'" *The New York Times*, September 17, 2001, p. A7.

3. Raphael Lewis, "Guard Recalls Suspects at Logan," *The Boston Globe*, September 16, 2001, p. A16.

4. Michael Dobbs, "Bin Laden's Air of Mystery," *The Washington Post*, September 12, 2001, <http://a188.g.akamaitech.net/f/188/920/2m/www.washingtonpost.com/wp-dyn/articles/A20783-2001Sep12.html> (September 16, 2001).

5. Hannah Bloch, et al., "Osama bin Laden: The Most Wanted Man in the World," *Time*, September 24, 2001, p. 58.

6. Evan Thomas, "A New Date of Infamy," *Newsweek Extra Edition*, Vol. CXXXVIII, No. 12-A, p. 25.

7. George W. Bush, "President Bush's Address on Terrorism Before a Joint Meeting of Congress," *The New York Times*, September 21, 2001, p. B4.

8. Michael Daly, "His Words Still Heal Us," *The New York Daily News*, September 16, 2001, p. 18.

9. "Love and Loss," *Newsweek*, September 24, 2001, p. 89.

10. George W. Bush, p. B4.

Glossary

air traffic controller—A person who directs and monitors different aircraft and keeps track of their progress by radar and radio.

airspace—The area above a geographic location.

casualty—A person who is killed or injured.

chaplain—A clergyman who is officially attached to an institution or military branch.

civilian—A person not enrolled in a military, police, or firefighting force.

debris—The remains of an object or structure after it has been destroyed.

extremist—Someone who interprets or views a particular issue in a very strict, narrow way that is usually very different from the viewpoints of most others.

fundamentalist—A person who lives according to a literal, inflexible interpretation of a set of principles.

hijack—To steal or take over control of a vehicle, usually through force or the threat of force.

Islam—A religion based on the teachings of the Prophet Muhammad. *Islam* is the Arabic word for *submission.* Those who practice Islam are often called *Muslims.*

jihad—A holy war in defense of Islam.

Muslim—An Arabic word that means "one who submits to God."

radical—Someone whose views differ greatly from the usual or traditional.

rubble—Large broken pieces of rock or stone.

terrorism—The systematic spread of fear (usually through violence) as a means toward attaining some goal.

triage—A process of sorting injured people into groups based on their needs and likely benefit from treatment.

Fridell, Ron. *Terrorism: Political Violence at Home and Abroad.* Berkeley Heights, N.J.: Enslow Publishers, Inc., 2001.

Life Magazine. *One Nation: America Remembers September 11, 2001.* New York: Little Brown & Company, 2001.

New York Magazine. *September 11, 2001, New York Attacked: A Record of Tragedy, Heroism, and Hope.* New York: Harry N. Abrams, 2001.

Sherrow, Victoria. *The World Trade Center Bombing: Terror in the Towers.* Berkeley Heights, N.J.: Enslow Publishers, Inc., 1998.

Waldman, Jackie. *America, September 11: The Courage to Give: The Triumph of the Human Spirit.* Berkeley, Calif.: Conari Press, 2001.

Internet Addresses

September 11 Web Archive
http://september11.archive.org/

A Tribute to Heroes
http://www.atributetoheroes.com

Dealing with a Terrorist Tragedy
http://www.kidshealth.org/breaking_news/tragedies.html

Portraits of Grief
http://www.nytimes.com/pages/national/portraits

How You Can Help

Here is a list of charitable organizations accepting contributions to help relief efforts and dispossessed families in the wake of the terrorist attacks of September 11, 2001:

The Twin Towers Fund
P.O. Box 26999
New York, NY 10087-6999

UFA Widows and
Childrens Fund
c/o UFA
204 E. 23rd Street
New York, NY 10010

New York Firefighters
9-11 Disaster Relief Fund
c/o IAFF
1750 New York Ave. N.W.
Washington, D.C. 20006

The American Red Cross
Disaster Relief Fund
Phone: 1-800-435-7669
http://www.redcross.org

The United Way of
New York City
2 Park Avenue
New York, NY 10016
Phone: 1-800-710-8002
http://www.uwnyc.org

Salvation Army
(mark donations either
"Twin Towers Relief" or
"Pentagon Relief")
P.O. Box C635
West Nyack, NY 10994-1739
Phone: 1-800-725-2769

New York City Firefighters
9-11 Disaster Relief Fund
Firehouse.com
9658 Baltimore Avenue,
Suite 350
College Park, MD 20740

Mercy Corps
Dept. W
U.S. Emergency Fund
P.O. Box 2669
Portland, OR 97208

Phone: 1-800-852-2100
http://www.mercycorps.org

R